It's another Quality Book from CGP

This book is for 11-14 year olds.

It contains lots of tricky questions designed
to make you sweat — because that's the only
way you'll get any better.

It's also got some daft bits in to try and make
the whole experience at least vaguely
entertaining for you.

What CGP is all about

Our sole aim here at CGP is to produce the highest quality
books — carefully written, immaculately presented
and dangerously close to being funny.

Then we work our socks off to get them out to you
— at the cheapest possible prices.

Useful bits for reference...

Definitions that are definitely worth knowing:

Photosynthesis — this process turns *carbon dioxide* and *water* into *glucose* and *oxygen* using *chlorophyll* and *sunlight*.

Respiration — this process turns *glucose* and *oxygen* into *energy* and produces *carbon dioxide* and *water*. Remember, respiration IS NOT the same as breathing.

Fertilisation — this is the joining together of the nucleus of the male sex cell and the nucleus of the female sex cell.

Carnivores — are animals which only eat other *animals*, never plants (the **Top Carnivore** is not eaten by anything else).

Herbivores — are animals which only eat plants, never animals.

Omnivores — are animals which eat both plants and other animals.

Invertebrates — are creatures which don't have a backbone.
Examples are *insects* and *spiders*.

Vertebrates — are creatures which have a backbone.
Examples are *fish*, *amphibians*, *reptiles*, *birds* and *mammals*.

Systems:

Digestive — breaks down the food so that it can be absorbed into the blood.

Respiratory — is for taking in oxygen and removing carbon dioxide.

Excretory — is for removing waste materials from the body.

Circulatory — transports nutrients and wastes around the body via the blood.

Reproductive — is for producing offspring.

Nervous — carries messages to and from the brain and muscles.

Gland — glands produce hormones which control things such as growth.

Skeletal — is for supporting the body and protecting vital organs like the brain.

Muscle — muscles attached to the bones contract and relax to allow movement.

Things to know the differences between:

Cross-Pollination and **Self-Pollination**.

Continuous Variation and **Discontinuous Variation**.

Consumers and **Producers**.

Other Handy Stuff:

The **seven essential food groups** are:
Carbohydrates, Proteins, Fats, Vitamins, Minerals, Roughage, Water.

Know the **differences** between *arteries*, *capillaries* and *veins*.

Plants need the *minerals*, *nitrates*, *phosphates* and *potassium* to grow properly.

Contents

A few pages have got a splodge like this one where bits have been taken out of the syllabus.

This stuff _shouldn't_ come up in the SATs, but it's still really important so we left it in.

Published by Coordination Group Publications Ltd.
Typesetting and layout by The Science Coordination Group
Illustrations by Sandy Gardner e-mail: illustrations@sandygardner.co.uk

Compiled by Paddy Gannon

ISBN 1 84146 639 5

Groovy website: www.cgpbooks.co.uk

Also thanks to CorelDRAW for providing one or two jolly bits of clipart.

Printed by Elanders Hindson, Newcastle upon Tyne.

Questions on the Microscope

Q1 Below is a typical microscope found in the lab. Join up the *label* with the correct *letter*.

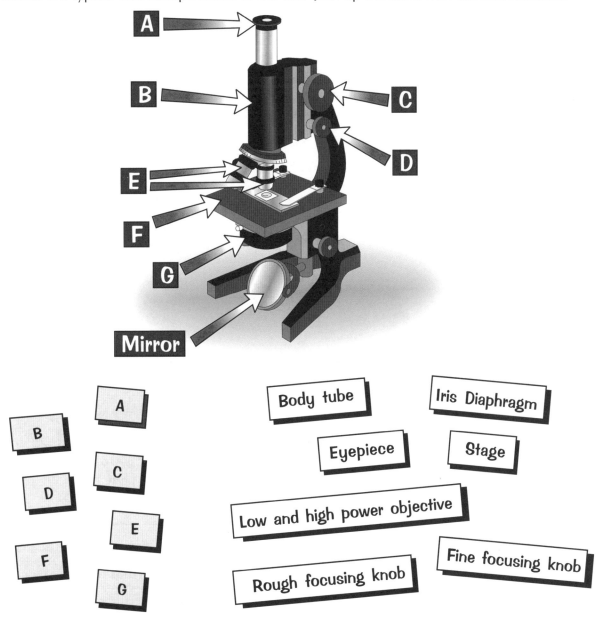

Body tube

Iris Diaphragm

Eyepiece

Stage

Low and high power objective

Rough focusing knob

Fine focusing knob

Q2 State what job each bit of the microscope does.

A ....

B ....

C ....

D ....

E ....

F ....

G ....

Questions on Life Processes

Q1 a) Complete the following *word search* using the words below.

N	O	I	T	C	U	D	O	R	P	E	R	G	N	C
W	U	V	P	G	Q	W	C	C	Q	N	C	O	C	D
V	E	L	J	I	L	B	K	G	P	E	I	M	N	U
T	D	K	T	H	E	B	Y	W	X	T	U	U	X	D
N	Z	O	C	L	Q	C	L	C	A	V	T	M	Z	H
E	S	C	L	J	X	M	R	R	T	R	M	K	F	V
M	F	C	J	I	G	E	I	W	I	Q	X	S	I	B
E	O	Y	Z	A	T	P	J	T	K	A	X	R	T	I
V	X	G	F	I	S	T	I	M	H	T	W	O	R	G
O	U	B	O	E	A	O	F	H	F	L	D	Y	T	I
M	S	N	R	I	N	N	P	E	I	K	J	P	B	H

Words:
reproduction
respiration
excretion
nutrition
movement
growth

b) Which *life process* is not in the word search above?

....

Q2 *Life Processes* are the things that both plants and animals do to be classified as being alive. Life Processes which are common to both plants and animals are shown in the table below. Match up the name of the *process* with its *meaning* by drawing a line between the two.

Life Process

Growth
Nutrition
Respiration
Excretion
Movement
Sensitivity
Reproduction

Meaning

The ability to produce more of its kind

The ability to move all or part of the organism

The increase in size and complexity of an organism

The ability of an organism to respond

The ability to take in oxygen and give out carbon dioxide to make energy

The removal of waste materials which the cells have made and may be poisonous

The ability to take in food or raw materials to support other life processes

Questions on Cells

Q1 The following diagrams show:

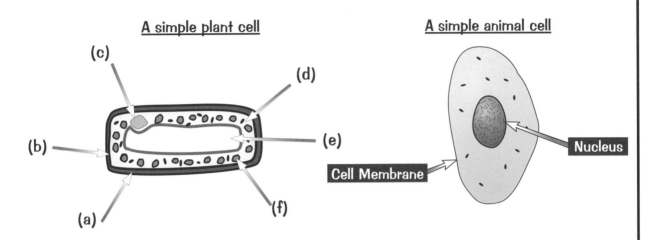

A simple plant cell

A simple animal cell

Name **a) - f)** in the above diagrams, then fill in the table below:

a) ....

d) ....

b) ....

e) ....

c) ....

f) ....

Both cells have	Only plant cells have
1)	1)
2)	2)
3)	3)

Q2 Which part of both cells passes on information to new cells?

....

Q3 Which part of the plant cell absorbs the energy from the Sun and uses it in photosynthesis?

....

Q4 Complete the table below by placing a tick in the boxes where the cell parts are present in the cells listed.

	Cytoplasm	Nucleus	Cell wall	Vacuole
Leaf mesophyll				
Sperm				

4

Questions on Cells

Q5

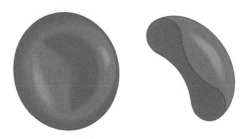

   a) What is the name of this type of cell?

   ....

   b) What job does it do?

   ....

   c) Why is it shaped with a dimple inside?

   ....

Q6

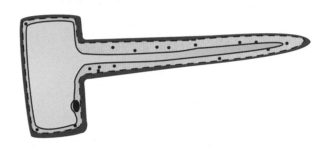

   a) This is a plant cell. What is it called?

   ....

   b) What job does it do?

   ....

   c) Where in the plant would you find this cell?

   ....

Q7   This is a nerve cell.

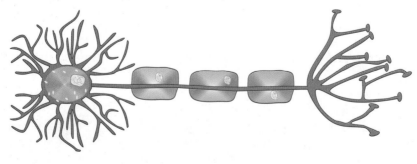

   What is the function of the nerve cell?

....

....

SECTION ONE — LIFE PROCESSES AND CELL ACTIVITY

Questions on Specialised Cells

Q1 Match each *cell structure* with the *cell function*.

Cell Structure

An epithelial cell with hairs on its outer membrane surface which waft or beat

Contains the red chemical substance called haemoglobin

Is a cell made with an extension (the tail)

Has a long cell cytoplasm and has many branches at the end / ends

Function (job)

Carries oxygen around the body

Carries information (impulses) round the body and joins other impulses

After a journey it joins with an egg cell

These cells are found in main body tubes like those near the lungs and help to trap germs and dust and clean the air

Q2 The drawings below (**a)** – **d)**) show a variety of animal and plant cells.

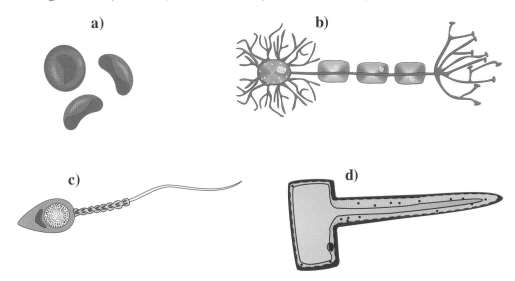

a)

b)

c)

d)

For each cell state :
i) the name *(type)* of cell.
ii) the life process(es) in which it is especially involved.

a) ....

....

b) ....

....

c) ....

....

d) ....

....

6

Questions on Plant Organs

Q1 From the diagram of the plant, name parts S to X and record their functions in the table below.

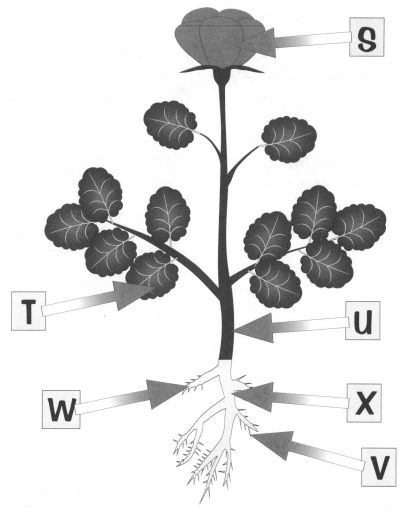

Letter	Name of Organ	Function
S		
T		
U		
V		
W		
X		

Questions on Plant Organs

Q2 Replace the letters in the chart below choosing from the following words to show the transport of water from the soil to the leaves:

| Shoot, | bud, | root, | flower, | root hair cell, | stem |

Soil → **A** → **B** → **C** → **D**

A ....   B ....

C ....   D ....

Q3 The following jumbled words are all parts of a plant.
Solve each word using the clues given.

a) *wrofle* – reproducing part of a plant ....

b) *plate* – part of a flower ....

c) *flea* – part which makes food ....

d) *mets* – support structure above the ground ....

e) *roto* – takes in water and minerals ....

Q4 a) What process takes place in the leaf of a plant?

....

b) Which two substances are used in this process?

....

c) Which substances are produced in this process?

....

d) Could this process take place in the dark? Explain your answer.

....

....

e) Write a word equation for this process. *(Words to use: Carbon/oxygen/sunlight/glucose/water/dioxide)*

_____ + _____ $\xrightarrow{(\text{_____})}$ _____ + _____

Questions on Human Organ Systems

Q1   Name the *systems* below which have some of their letters omitted.
There are some *clues* to help you.

   a)   This is the system which includes the *heart, blood* and *vessels*

       c _ _ c u l _ t _ _ y .

   b)   This is the system which involves the *lungs* and *airways*

       _ _ _ p i _ _ t _ _ _ .

   c)   This is the system which involves the *stomach* and the *intestine*

       d _ _ e _ _ i _ _ .

   d)   This is the system for producing offspring

       _ _ p r _ _ u _ _ i v _ .

Q2   Complete the table below by naming the organs **a)** to **e)** and for each one state in which system they are included.

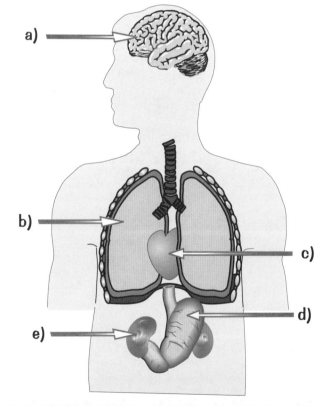

Letter	Organ	System
a		
b		
c		
d		
e		

Questions on Human Organ Systems

Q3 Match the *organ* in Box A with the *function* (job) in Box B by writing the correct letter next to the numbers listed below. *(E.g. 1) t) or 2) u)).*

1) ......
2) ......
3) ......
4) ......
5) ......
6) ......

A	B
1) lungs	p) to provide information about the environment
2) brain	q) to take oxygen in/to remove carbon dioxide from the body
3) stomach	r) to allow movement
4) kidneys	s) to control and organise the body's activities
5) muscles	t) to digest (break down) food
6) sense organs (eyes, nose, etc.)	u) to purify the blood and remove waste products

Q4 a) What do we call a part of the body with a special function?

....

b) What do we call a group of organs which work together to carry out a particular function?

....

Q5 Look at the four diagrams of *human body systems* and state the name of each system (there are two in diagram D).

A) ....

B) ....

C) ....

D) ....

....

A

Brain
Optic nerve
Nerve
Spinal cord

B

Gullet
Stomach
Large Intestine
Small Intestine
Anus

C

Heart
Artery
Vein

D

Windpipe
Lung
Diaphram
a

Kidney
Ureter
Bladder
b

SECTION ONE — LIFE PROCESSES AND CELL ACTIVITY

Questions on Nutrition

Q1 a) Complete the table which shows the _function_ (job) of each food group.

Carbohydrates		Fats		
	Used for growth and repair		Usually needed in small amounts to help make certain parts of the body	A large group of substances needed in small amounts to prevent many diseases like scurvy

b) What does the word '_nutrition_' mean?

....

....

c) _Water is not a food but without it a person would die within several days. Even though water cannot be stored in the body it must be taken in and lost every day._ State what _percentage_ of the body is water.

....

d) What is a _deficiency disease?_

....

....

e) What problem would occur if you did not include enough fresh fruit and vegetables in your diet?

....

....

Q2 _Peter is going on a 50 mile sponsored walk and he knows it is going to take him a long time. He really likes sausages for his tea so he thinks it would be a good idea to take some to give him lots of energy._ He puts all the following food on the table ready to pack.

a) Why should he not take the sausages for energy on his walk?

....

....

b) Which _main ingredient_ is missing from his pack?

....

Questions on Nutrition

Q3 Study the three pie charts showing the food groups of breakfast cereals.

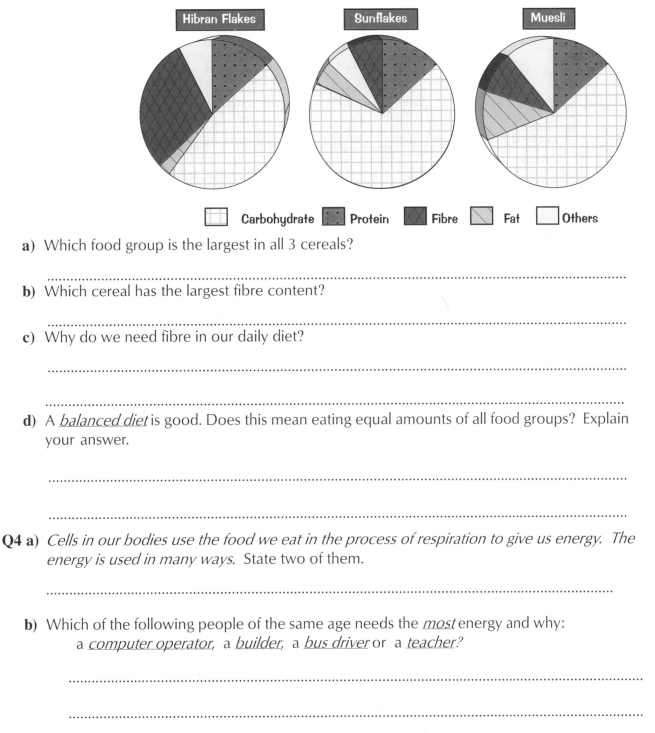

Hibran Flakes   Sunflakes   Muesli

☐ Carbohydrate ⬚ Protein ◆ Fibre ◢ Fat ☐ Others

   a) Which food group is the largest in all 3 cereals?

   ....

   b) Which cereal has the largest fibre content?

   ....

   c) Why do we need fibre in our daily diet?

   ....

   ....

   d) A _balanced diet_ is good. Does this mean eating equal amounts of all food groups? Explain
   your answer.

   ....

   ....

Q4 a) *Cells in our bodies use the food we eat in the process of respiration to give us energy. The*
   energy is used in many ways. State two of them.

   ....

   b) Which of the following people of the same age needs the _most_ energy and why:
   a _computer operator,_ a _builder,_ a _bus driver_ or a _teacher?_

   ....

   ....

   c) Fill in the sentence by choosing appropriate words from the list below.

respiration	growth	food	nuclear power station
fuel	nutrition	substance	repair	energy

   Food is used as a _____ for the process of _____

   and as a raw material for _____ and _____ .

Questions on Digestion

Q1   Complete the introductory sentences below with words from the word list (some words will be left over).

small,   insoluble,   egestion,   small intestine,   small,   large intestine,   soluble, large colon,   digestion,   nerves,   bloodstream,   enzymes,   large

The process of _____ is the breakdown of food into _____ substances,

and the passage into the _____. The food molecules are too _____ to

pass through the walls of the _____ and need to be broken down by special

chemicals called _____.

Q2 a) Use the diagram of the *digestive system* to fill in the chart showing the names and functions of A to F.

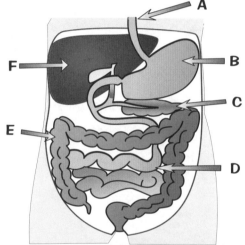

Letter	Name	Function
A		
B		
C		
D		
E		
F		

b) Match each *digestive part* to the *enzymes* it produces by drawing a line between the two.

Digestive Part	Enzyme(s) produced
mouth	Proteases in acid, which digests protein
stomach	Salivary amylase
pancreas	Protease, carbohydrase and lipase

SECTION TWO — HUMANS AS ORGANISMS PART ONE

Questions on Digestion

Q3 *The pupils in Priesthorp High School performed an experiment to try to show why <u>digestion</u> must take place. They set up the experiment as below using <u>visking tubing</u>, which is <u>semi-permeable</u> and achieved the set of results given.* Use the results to answer the questions.

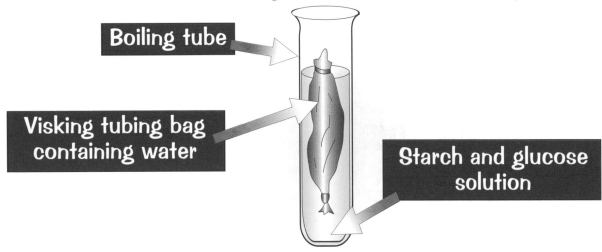

Water inside visking tubing	Starch present	Glucose present
At start	no	no
After 25 mins	no	yes

a) Can starch *pass through* the visking tubing? Explain your answer.

....

....

....

b) Explain why glucose could pass through the visking tubing.

....

....

....

c) What *part of our body* acts like the visking tubing?

....

d) In the experiment which substance in the body does the water represent?

....

e) What is the starch and glucose mixture supposed to represent?

....

Questions on Digestion

Q4 Find the missing words in the diagrams, which show _enzyme action_ on large molecules.

Digestion of Carbohydates

| A large starch molecule is made up of many (a)_____ molecules | → | Starch is broken down by (b)_____ enzymes | → | to give (c)_____ and other simple sugars |

Digestion of Proteins

| A protein molecule consists of many (d)_____ molecules | → | Proteins are broken down by (e)____ enzymes | → | to give individual (f) _____ molecules |

Digestion of Fats

| A large fat molecule is made up of (g)____ and (h)____ | → | Fats are broken down by (i)____ enzymes | → | to give individual (j) _____ and (k)_____ molecules |

(a) ....

(b) ....

(c) ....

(d) ....

(e) ....

(f) ....

(g) ....

(h) ....

(i) ....

(j) ....

(k) ....

Q5 _Once the food has been broken down into smaller soluble molecules it needs to be absorbed from the alimentary canal into the blood._

a) In which _structure_ does this process of absorption take place?

....

b) Name the special structures we find in 'a)' that aid absorption.

....

c) State two ways in which the structures named in 'b)' are adapted for their job.

....

....

Questions on Absorption and the Kidneys

Q1 Where do the particles of digested food go?

....

Q2 What is the name of the process which takes digested food through the small intestine wall?

....

Q3 State three reasons why *villi* are ideal for absorption.

....

....

....

Q4 a) Circle the word which means the removal of *undigested food*.

excretion , *renal* , *egestion* , *contraction* , *filtered*.

b) Which word is the name of the organ from which waste undigested materials leave the body? ....

c) Name an organ which excretes **i)** *carbon dioxide* and **ii)** *water*.

i) ....

ii) ....

Q5 Some of the foods are *stored* in your body after absorption. Give the names of two digested food substances, state where they're stored and what they're used for.

1) ....

....

2) ....

....

Q6 When the kidneys work they *absorb* all the useful and all the waste products, filter out the waste and put the useful products back into the blood.

a) State two *useful substances* which the kidneys might absorb again.

....

....

b) Give the name of a *waste substance* from the blood which the kidneys get rid of.

....

16

Questions on the Circulatory System

Taken ou
of the curriculum
but still importar

Q1   Complete the introduction by filling in the gaps, using the words in the box.

oxygen	nutrients	grow	heart	transport	waste

Blood is the _____ system of the body. It carries _____ and

_____ to all parts of the body. It is pumped round the body by the

_____ . It also takes away _____ products.

Q2 a) The following diagrams are of the *cells* found in the *blood*.
Complete the table below by naming them and giving the function of each.

 A
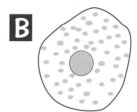 B
 C

Letter	Name	Function
A		
B		
C		

b) Explain two ways in which *white cells* work.

....

....

....

....

c) Other than these three types of cells, what makes up the blood?

....

....

SECTION TWO — HUMANS AS ORGANISMS PART ONE

Taken out
of the curriculum
but still important

Questions on the Circulatory System

Q3 Draw in *lines* to match the statements on the left with the information on the right.

Plasma

Capillaries

Red blood cells

White blood cells

Antibodies

Platelets

Heart

Fight against disease occurring

Can be produced by a certain type of blood cell

Contain haemoglobin

Help the blood to clot and so prevents invaders

Narrow blood tubes

The body's blood pump

The liquid portion of the blood

Q4 Which cells in the blood do not have a *nucleus?*

....

Q5 What is the name of the pigment which makes red blood cells red?

....

Q6 Look at the three blood vessels below. For each one, name the vessel and explain its features.

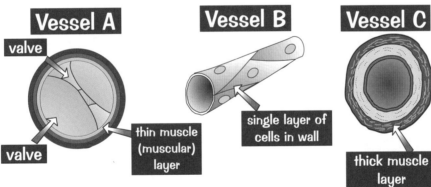

Vessel A — valve — thin muscle (muscular) layer — valve

Vessel B — single layer of cells in wall

Vessel C — thick muscle layer

Vessel A ....

....

....

Vessel B ....

....

Vessel C ....

....

SECTION TWO — HUMANS AS ORGANISMS PART ONE

Questions on the Circulatory System

Taken out of the curriculum but still important

Q7 a) Which side of your heart (when facing the front), left or right, contains deoxygenated blood (blood without oxygen)?

....

b) Which side, left or right, puts the most pressure on the blood?

....

Q8 Look at the diagram to the right.

a) Starting at B place the letters that label it in order to show the *complete flow* of blood into and out of the heart.

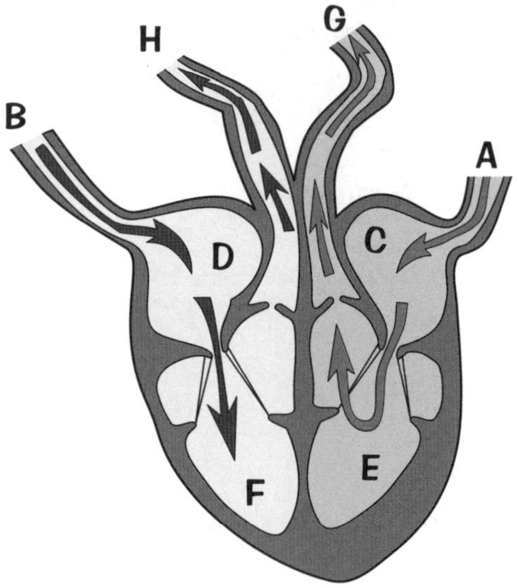

B → __ → __ → __ → __ → __ → __ → __

b) Label four valves on the diagram of the heart.

c) Why are valves needed?

....

d) Which blood vessels, *arteries* or *veins*, carry blood away from the heart?

....

e) Complete the following sentences using the letters from the heart diagram above.

.... is the part of the heart where the deoxygenated blood comes first.

.... is the main artery in the body and carries blood with oxygen away from the heart.

.... is the left top part of the heart.

.... is the blood vessel which carries blood with carbon dioxide from the heart to the lungs to pick up oxygen and remove the carbon dioxide.

.... is the blood vessel which brings back blood with oxygen from the lungs to the heart.

.... is the part of the heart with the thickest walls to put the blood under the most pressure.

.... is the blood vessel which carries blood from the tissues to the heart.

Questions on the Skeleton, Joints and Muscles

Q1   Fill in the missing words. Some letters have already been put in to help you.

The <u>b</u> _ _ _ _ in your skeleton protect many important <u>o</u> _ _ _ _ _ in your body.

Bones also allow <u>m</u> _ _ _ _ _ _ _ to occur at joints and they also <u>s</u> _ _ _ _ _ _ t

the entire body.

Q2 a) Using the diagram below place the parts in the correct order to form a figure of a skeleton.

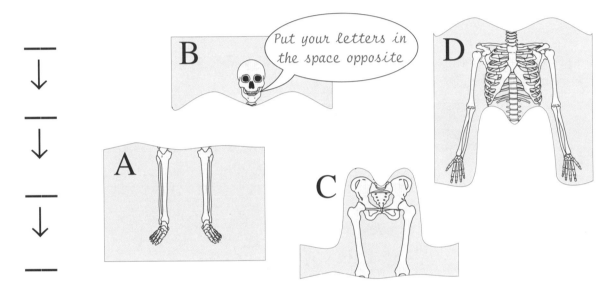

Put your letters in the space opposite

b) From the skeleton diagram complete the following table of *names* and *functions*.

Clue	Name	Function
1) The main head bone.		
2) The bones which are involved when we breathe.		
3) The column at the back of the body.		
4) The upper arm bone that is not funny if you lift things in the wrong way.		
5) There's a pair of them, and they have long bones and large joints.		

Questions on the Skeleton, Joints and Muscles

Q3 a) Why is it important that bones are **i)** *strong* and **ii)** *light?*

   i) ....

   ....

   ii) ....

   ....

  b) Why are two pairs of ribs called the *floating ribs?*

   ....

Q4 a) From the list below name the *pair of substances* which are needed for healthy bones, and name a food which contains both.

calcium and vitamin C	vitamin D and calcium
iron and vitamin D	vitamin C and iron

   ....

  b) The two diagrams show a *male* and *female* pelvis. Look carefully at the two diagrams and state which is which and why.

A   B

   ....

   ....

   ....

   ....

Q5 Complete this paragraph using the words in the box.

fluid	cartilage	joint	ligaments

Wherever bones meet a _____ is formed. Bones are held

together by strong fibres called _____. The bones are

prevented from rubbing on each other and wearing away by smooth

_____ and there is also a _____ which fills the joint.

Questions on the Skeleton, Joints and Muscles

Q6 Look at the *knee joint* diagram opposite and answer the questions which follow it.

a) *The knee joint is a 'freely movable' joint.*

Name **i)** a slightly movable joint, **ii)** an immovable joint

i) ....

ii) ....

b) Which part of the diagram represents the *cartilage?*

....

c) Why is it necessary that cartilage is present in all moving joints?

....

....

d) Explain what might be the cause of a rugby player finding it painful to bend over in scrums.

....

....

Q7 a) Look at the diagram and name the labelled parts which show the arm as a hinge joint. Use the words in the box below to help you.

Radius	Biceps muscle	Triceps muscle
Ulna	Humerus	Elbow

A ....

B ....

C ....

D ....

E ....

F ....

b) A *flexor muscle* bends a joint; which is the flexor muscle in the elbow joint?

....

c) An *extensor muscle* straightens a joint; give the name of one in the elbow joint.

....

d) Name the structures which join (**A**) and (**B**) and all muscles to the bone.

....

Questions on Growing Up

Q1 Fill in the spaces from the word list below to show how humans *develop*.

sex organs	ovaries	sperm	puberty	reproduce
eggs	testes	sexual	genetic	fertilisation

Children, like all young animals cannot _____ because their _____ have

not fully developed. In order to produce offspring the female _____ must

produce _____ and the male _____ must produce _____. The

process of reproduction in humans is called _____ reproduction where the

material in the male sex cells combines with that in the female sex cells when _____

occurs. The stage of life when human sex organs begin to develop is called _____.

Q2 *During this important stage of life many physical and emotional changes occur which are controlled by hormones carried in the blood.*

a) Look carefully at the statements below. In each box put either an **M**, **F** or **B** to show whether the statement applies to males, females or both.

A) The testes start to make sperm. ☐   G) Your emotions change a lot. ☐

B) The male sex hormone is made. ☐   H) Erections happen during this time. ☐

C) Hair grows around the sex organs. ☐   I) You often feel and think differently. ☐

D) The female sex hormone is made. ☐   J) The hips become rounder. ☐

E) A small amount of blood is lost   K) The breasts develop. ☐

every month when the lining of   L) An egg is released once a month. ☐

the uterus breaks down. This is   M) The ovaries produce eggs. ☐

known as a period. ☐   N) Glands make hormones to start

F) The body becomes more   the body changes. ☐

muscular and the shoulders   O) Hair grows under the armpits. ☐

broaden. ☐   P) The sex organs begin to grow. ☐

b) What is the name of the period of life between puberty and adulthood?

....

....

Questions on Growing Up

Q3 The following are very important key words regarding _Growth and Changing_.
Explain the meaning of each word below.

puberty

....

....

....

ovaries

....

testes

....

sex hormones

....

....

adulthood

....

....

....

Q4 Find the following seven words in the word search connected with this section on Growing Up.

Sex hormones		Ovaries	Testes
Physical	Puberty	Adulthood	Adolescence

S	E	N	O	M	R	O	H	X	E	S
T	H	I	S	I	S	H	A	R	D	T
X	A	D	U	L	T	H	O	O	D	Y
J	B	A	D	C	E	F	V	G	U	H
J	P	H	Y	S	I	C	A	L	K	L
T	M	I	N	P	O	Q	R	S	T	U
V	E	W	E	X	Y	Z	I	A	C	E
B	A	S	C	P	U	B	E	R	T	Y
F	I	B	T	G	I	B	S	H	I	P
J	A	B	K	E	G	L	I	M	B	S
E	C	N	E	C	S	E	L	O	D	A

Questions on the Menstrual Cycle

Q1   *The menstrual cycle concerns egg release which occurs every month in females.* In the following set of sentences fill in the missing words from the box below.

| menstrual cycle | uterus | fertilised | bacteria |
| month | ovary | blood | menstruation |

The egg cell is released normally from an _____ once a

_____. Each time an egg cell is released the _____ gets

ready to grow a baby. A thick lining full of _____ vessels slowly

develops. If the egg is _____ it passes into the uterus and becomes

attached to it. The uterus grows a fresh new lining every time an egg is

released because the environment in the uterus provides excellent

conditions for _____ to grow and so it must be replaced. If the

egg is not fertilised the breakdown of the uterus lining occurs and this is

called _____. The whole sequence of making a new uterus

lining and an egg is called the _____.

Q2   Match each term on the left with the explanation on the right.

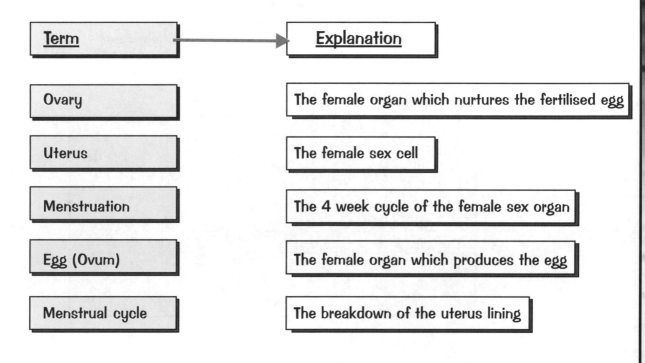

| Term | | Explanation |

| Ovary | | The female organ which nurtures the fertilised egg |

| Uterus | | The female sex cell |

| Menstruation | | The 4 week cycle of the female sex organ |

| Egg (Ovum) | | The female organ which produces the egg |

| Menstrual cycle | | The breakdown of the uterus lining |

Questions on the Menstrual Cycle

Q3   Study the following diagrams showing the menstrual cycle.

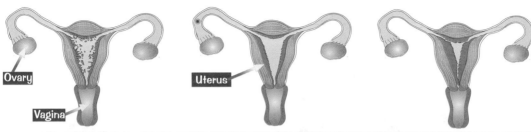

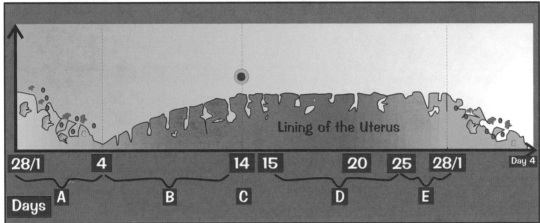

Key
- ▬ = blood and lining
- ⊙ = egg released from ovary

For each sentence below, put the corresponding letter from the diagram in the box.

1) The lining of the *uterus* is very thick and full of blood. ☐

2) The lining of the uterus builds up. ☐

3) The egg is released from the *ovary*. ☐

4) The egg is travelling down the *oviduct* to be fertilised. ☐

5) The thick lining of the uterus breaks down and blood flows out (menstruation). ☐

Q4 a) Why does the lining of the uterus need to become thick?

....

....

   b) How long does it take the uterus lining to build up again after menstruation?

....

   c) At which point in the menstrual cycle is the egg released?

....

Questions on Having a Baby

Q1 *In order to have a baby the male and female* <u>sex cell nuclei</u> *with* <u>genetic information</u> *must join. You must understand the male and female reproductive organs and what they do.*

a) Complete the table below:

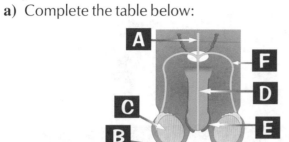
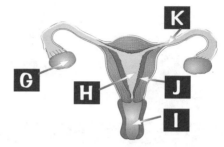

Male reproductive organs			Female reproductive organs		
		Name			**Name**
	A			G	
	B			H	
	C			I	
	D			J	
	E			K	
	F				

b) Following the release of sperm into the vagina during intercourse, what must happen for an egg to be fertilised?

....

....

c) Where is the female egg fertilised?

....

d) What type of *genetic information* does a new baby contain?

....

....

Q2 a) Which process places millions of sperm in the female?

....

b) What happens to all the other sperm when a sperm enters the egg?

....

....

c) Where does the genetic information in a fertilised egg come from?

....

....

Questions on Having a Baby

Q3 a) Once the egg is fertilised and it implants itself in the uterus lining, it must have room to grow. There are 3 other things that it requires. Name these.

....

b) Place the following diagrams in the correct order to show the *development* of a *fertilised egg*.

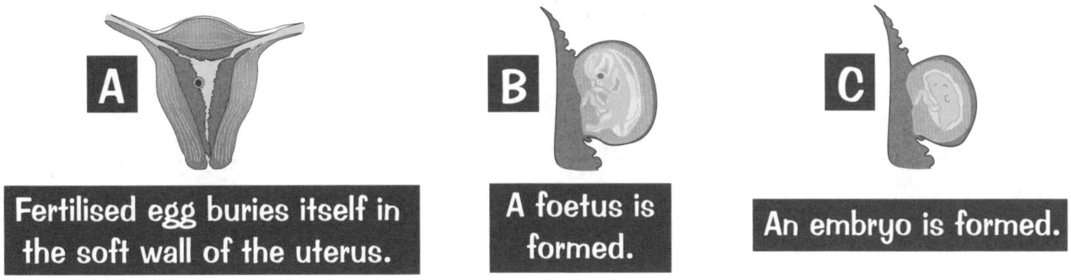

Fertilised egg buries itself in the soft wall of the uterus.

A foetus is formed.

An embryo is formed.

___ → ___ → ___

c) State the first structure that the fertilised egg makes.

....

d) What is the word which describes a female carrying an embryo?

....

e) Is it true that periods occur as normal after an egg is fertilised? Explain your answer.

....

....

Q4 The diagram to the right shows a *foetus* developing in a uterus. Name the labelled parts on the diagram from the word list.

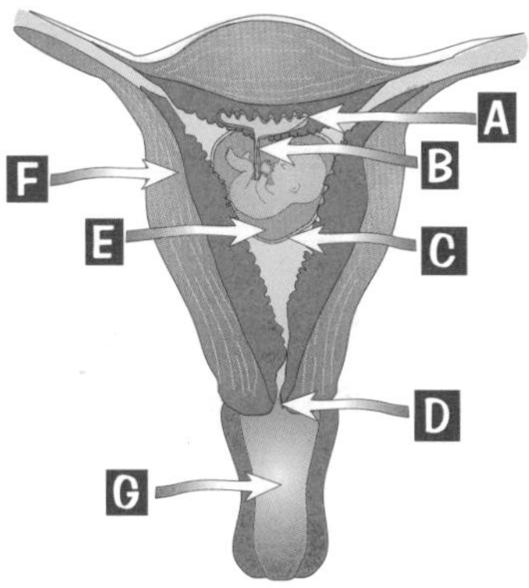

Word list : cervix, amnion, uterus, placenta, vagina, amniotic fluid, umbilical cord.

A ....
B ....
C ....
D ....
E ....
F ....
G ....

Q5 The diagram to the right shows the blood supply relationship between the mother's blood and that of the foetus.

Is it true that the mother's blood mixes with the foetus's blood? If not, state what does happen?

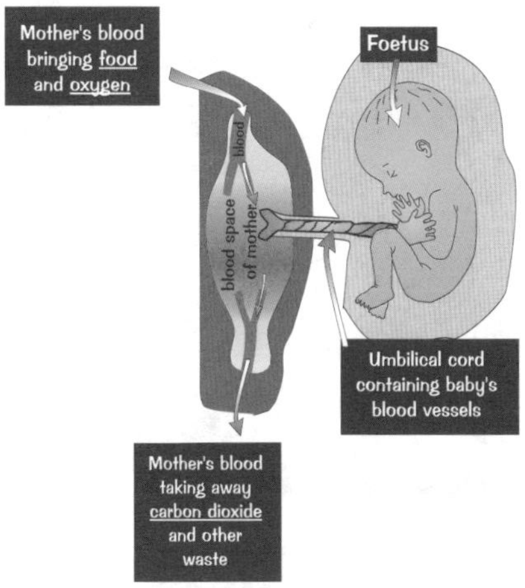

....

....

Questions on Having a Baby

Q6 a) How many months after fertilisation is the birth of the baby?

....

b) Does the diagram in Q4 show the foetus ready for birth? If not, why?

....

....

....

c) What must be cut to separate the baby from the mother after it is born?

....

....

....

d) What is left inside the mother after delivery? What happens to it?

....

....

Q7 Complete the word search by finding the following *key words:*

> pregnancy, gestation, reproduction, intercourse, menstruation, fertilisation, oviduct, placenta, embryo, uterus, ovum, sperm, penis, vagina.

a	i	r	g	o	v	a	g	i	n	a	a	u	t	t	x	o	g
i	n	d	e	x	b	c	d	e	f	o	g	h	t	i	j	v	k
f	t	l	m	p	n	o	p	q	r	s	v	t	u	e	v	u	w
e	e	x	y	m	r	x	a	b	c	d	e	i	f	g	r	m	h
r	r	i	j	e	k	o	l	m	n	o	p	q	d	r	s	u	t
t	c	u	g	n	v	w	d	x	y	z	a	b	c	u	d	e	s
i	o	f	e	s	g	h	p	u	i	j	k	l	m	n	c	o	p
l	u	q	s	t	e	r	r	s	c	t	u	v	s	w	x	t	y
i	r	z	t	r	m	a	e	b	c	t	d	e	f	p	g	h	i
s	s	j	a	u	b	k	g	p	e	n	i	s	l	m	e	n	o
a	e	p	t	a	r	q	n	r	s	t	u	o	v	w	x	r	y
t	z	a	i	t	y	b	a	c	d	e	f	g	n	h	i	j	m
i	k	l	o	i	o	m	n	o	p	q	r	s	t	u	v	w	x
o	y	z	n	o	a	b	c	c	d	p	l	a	c	e	n	t	a
n	e	f	g	n	h	i	y	j	k	l	m	n	o	p	q	r	s

Questions on Breathing

The <u>respiratory system</u> is the name given to the system made up from the body's breathing organs. Oxygen is taken in from the air and carbon dioxide and water vapour breathed out.

Q1 In the diagram below label the <u>breathing organs</u> by placing the correct letters in the table opposite the name.

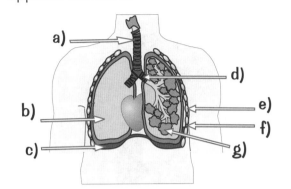

Name	Letter
Lung	
Windpipe (trachea)	
Bronchus (plural: bronchi)	
Alveoli	
Diaphragm	
Ribs	
Rib muscles (intercostal muscles)	

Q2 Use the following words to fill in the missing spaces:

| blood | lungs | breathing | oxygen | air | carbon dioxide | energy |

The _____ we need to stay alive comes from the _____ . The

waste gas, _____ , and water vapour go out of our body.

This total process is called _____ .

The important gas we take in enters our _____ and is used with sugar in

the cells to release _____ .

Q3 Match up the sentences on the left with those on the right to show how air is brought in and out of the lungs in the process of breathing. *(One is done for you)*

Rib muscles contract	Rib cage moves downwards and inwards
Diaphragm contracts	Diaphragm becomes dome-shaped i.e. moves upwards
More space is formed in the chest	Air is forced out from the chest space
Rib muscles relax	Rib cage moves upwards and outwards
Diaphragm relaxes	Diaphragm becomes flatter
Less space is left in the chest	Air enters to fill the extra room

Questions on Breathing

Q4   *A piece of apparatus was set up as shown in the diagram. The idea was to show how breathing works. You get to explain how it works by answering the questions below.*

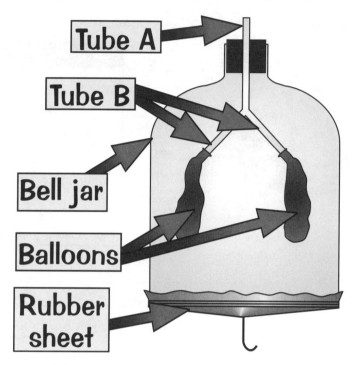

Tube A

Tube B

Bell jar

Balloons

Rubber sheet

a) Which *organ* in the body do the balloons represent?

....

b) Which main tube (A) brings air into and out of the body?

....

c) What is the name of the tubes (B) which take air in and out of the lungs?

....

d) Which *two muscles* control breathing?

....

e) Name the muscle which the *rubber sheet* represents.

....

f) What structure in the body does the bell jar represent?

....

g) What happens to the balloons when the rubber sheet is pulled downwards?

....

....

h) What part of the breathing process is this?

....

Questions on Breathing

Q5 The diagram shows the end of the small tubes — the *bronchioles* in the lungs

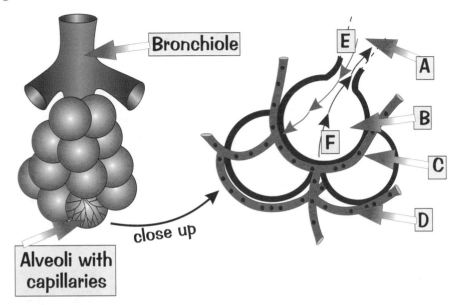

Bronchiole

Alveoli with capillaries

close up

a) What is the name of the small tube (A)?

....

b) The small tube (A) ends in a tiny sac. What is the tiny sac (B) called?

....

c) The lung has to exchange the two gases *carbon dioxide* and *oxygen* from the cells. Name the part of the body (C) in which the exchange occurs.

....

d) There are certain cells (D) in blood which are very important in this exchange process. State what they are called.

....

e) Why does the lung have many of these air sacs?

....

....

....

f) What do the *alveoli* and *blood capillaries* have in common, and why?

....

....

....

g) Name gases (E) and (F) which enter and leave the lungs.

....

Questions on Smoking

Q1 Write the introduction to this section yourself by placing the words from the word list into the paragraph below:

windpipe	lungs	air	cilia	mucus	swallowed	clean

The way in which we make sure we get good _____ into our _____

is to _____ it first. To do this our _____ has special cells which

produce sticky _____ which trap dust. There are also tiny hairs called

_____ to take the mixture back to the throat where it can be _____ .

Q2 *The following diagram shows the <u>windpipe</u> and the parts which are present to clean the air in a <u>healthy</u> person.* Match each boxed fact to the correct letter in the diagram.

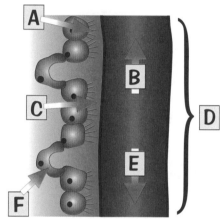

1) Thin layer of sticky mucus

2) Movement of mucus and dirt up to the throat

3) Cells with cilia move the mucus

4) Goblet cell to make mucus

5) Movement of clean air down to the lungs

6) The windpipe

1) ___   2) ___   3) ___   4) ___   5) ___   6) ___

Q3 The following diagram shows the windpipe of a *smoker*.

a) State two things which are different from those in a healthy person.

....

....

b) If *bacteria* are not trapped before air enters the lungs they can cause an infection. State the name of this disease.

....

c) When mucus collects in the tubes to the lungs it gives rise to an unpleasant action. Name this.

....

d) Give one reason why an unborn baby's development might be affected if the mother smokes during pregnancy.

....

....

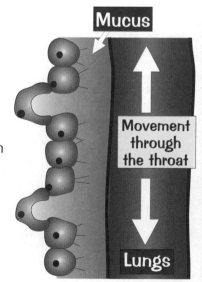

Mucus

Movement through the throat

Lungs

Questions on Smoking

Q4 *The normal process for cells in the body is to grow, then <u>divide</u>, and so replace cells which are too old.*

a) Tobacco smoke contains chemicals which make cells divide too much and a serious disease may occur. Name this disease.

....

b) Apart from the serious disease in **a)** name two more diseases which have connections with smoking.

....

....

c) What is '*passive*' smoking?

....

....

d) Which poisonous gas that comes out of car exhausts is present in the smoke from smokers?

....

Q5 The following words are *key words* in this section. See if you can find them in the word search below.

> Bronchitis, inhaled, exhaled, alveoli, emphysema, nicotine, mucus, cilia, windpipe, tar, tumour, passive smoking, bronchioles, carbon monoxide, haemoglobin, bacteria.

```
F B A C T E R I A S I E Y A I C
R T Z B C N Y G H R T L H D T H
T C L Q E I C E M P H Y S E M A
E J D R W T L E I L O E V L A E
N G N I K O M S E V I S S A P M
D M I J X C I L I A T E M H C O
T B T L E I N E Z N B I Z X B G
C A R B O N M O N O X I D E N L
R S P O T T V T L H M I L H M O
M J W I N D P I P E G K S C G B
Q N J D R C L A R Q O E R Q O I
I B R O N C H I O L E S F T Z N
R Y P E T T V I N H A L E D M A
M J V R U O M U T E G K S R G K
Q N J D R B L A R I O E R Q O E
F M R F W T M U C U S C F T Z X
```

34

Questions on Respiration

Q1 Use the *word list* below to fill the blank spaces.

> movement,   respiration,   energy,   growth,
> glucose,   carbon dioxide,   reproduction.

In this section we show how _____ is oxidised to

produce _____ . This process is called _____

and the glucose is broken down to make _____ ,

water and energy. All living things need energy for processes such as

_____ , _____ , and _____ .

Q2 Respiration is a *chemical reaction*.

a) What are the *reactants* (the bits you start with)?

....

b) What are the *chemical products?*

....

....

c) What else is produced? Name three things it is used for.

....

....

....

....

d) Use the letters to fill in the boxes in the diagram describing respiration.

> A=Air   D=Glucose
> B=Carbon Dioxide   E= Food   __Example:__   G=Energy
> C=Water   F=Oxygen

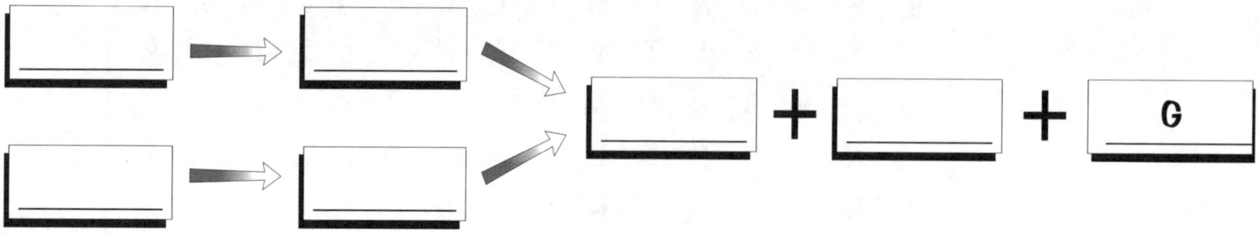

35

Questions on Respiration

Q3 The following *experiment* was set up to show the breakdown of sugar by heat:

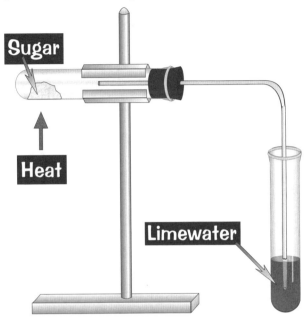

a) Why is *sugar* used in this experiment?

....

....

....

b) When the sugar is heated what happens to the *limewater*?

....

c) What does this prove?

....

d) Which process in the body does this experiment simulate?

....

e) Which gas must be used in this process and why?

....

....

f) If this process were taking place in our body cells what would be the most important product made? Explain why this is so.

....

....

....

....

Questions on Respiration

Q4   *Glucose molecules have energy and some of this is released during respiration.*

a) What in the body uses the energy released from glucose?

....

b) Does the energy have to be used up immediately? Explain your answer.

....

c) Write an equation for respiration using the following words: *(carbon dioxide, oxygen, water, energy, glucose.)*

           +   →   +   +

....

d) The glucose molecule contains carbon, hydrogen, and oxygen. In respiration it is oxidised (reacts with oxygen) to form three products. Name the products and state which are wastes and which are useful.

....

....

....

Q5   *Plants get their energy from the <u>sun</u> and gases in the <u>atmosphere</u>, and we know that the atmosphere is not pure oxygen but a mixture of gases.*

a) Name the three gases that are most common in the atmosphere.

....

....

Sometimes our muscles work very hard, especially if we are athletes. This is when oxygen is used at an especially high rate to make vast amounts of energy.

b) Which cells in the body carry the oxygen around for respiration?

....

c) What happens if the body cannot work fast enough to supply as much oxygen as is needed for the breaking down of glucose?

....

....

....

....

Questions on Respiration

Q6a) What type of _living organisms_ does respiration take place in?

....

b) Which _cells_ does respiration occur in?

....

c) What is the important and very useful product of respiration?

....

d) Explain why this product is so important.

....

....

....

Q7 The _key words_ for this section are listed below:

> aerobic respiration, glucose, carbon dioxide, energy,
> enzymes, water, oxygen, nitrogen, limewater, aerobics.

a) Fill the gaps in the puzzle below.

A) _ _ _ o _ _ c r _ _ p _ _ _ t _ _ _,

B) e _ _ _ m _ s,

C) _ n _ _ g _,

D) _ a _ _ o _ _ i _ _ i _ _,

E) _ _ t _ r,

F) o _ _ g _ _,

G) _ l _ c _ s _,

H) n _ _ r _ _ e _,

I) _ i _ _ w _ _ e _,

J) _ e _ o _ i _ _.

b) One word in the list above referred to a type of exercise where oxygen completely breaks down glucose and helps the body work hard. Which word is it?

....

Questions on Health

It's important to know about <u>drugs</u> because if they are not properly controlled they can damage our health. The <u>only people</u> we should trust to prescribe us with drugs are our doctors.

Q1 Complete the following table in the required places using the names and information boxes by matching the letters and numbers.

Name of drug	Facts about drug
(a)	Very expensive, addictive; leads to a sense of well-being; can cause death
Barbiturates	(b)
(c)	Causes hallucinations or 'trips' and dizzy actions
(d)	Causes a relaxed feeling or 'high'; makes driving or operating machinery hazardous; can cause mental problems
Cocaine	(e)

1) Can reduce anxiety but may cause death

2) LSD

3) Can speed up the brain and increase alertness but may cause depression or death

4) Heroin

5) Cannabis

a) ___ b) ___ c) ___ d) ___ e) ___

Q2 What do we mean when we say the following things about drugs:
a) they are *addictive?*

....

....

b) they have *side effects?*

....

....

Q3 *<u>Alcohol</u> is easy to buy legally if you are over 18 years of age, but it can damage your health if taken without care, and it <u>is</u> a drug.*

a) Circle the *<u>group of drugs</u>* that alcohol belongs to, given that it slows down the activity of the brain.

hallucinogen   stimulant   depressant   tranquiliser

b) Which *<u>two organs</u>* of the body can be damaged by drinking too much alcohol?

....

c) Explain how the affects of alcohol make drink driving so dangerous.

....

....

....

Questions on Health

Q4 a) __ __ __ __ __ __ __ __ abuse refers to the practise of inhaling the fumes from a variety of substances.

b) Name three of these substances which are commonly found in households.

....

c) Circle **i)** In *pencil*, the effects 'glue sniffing' has and

ii) In *pen*, the damage it can do to the body.

i)	Makes you sleepy	Makes you light headed	Gives hallucinations	Helps you to relax
ii)	Stops the process of digestion	Can damage brain and lungs	Can cause damage to the eyes	Can cause damage to the nervous system

Q5 Match each diagram of a substance containing a drug with the diagram of the organ which it is most likely to damage.

1 __
2 __
3 __

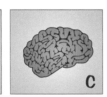

Q6 a) Fill the missing words below.

B _ _ _ _ _ _ _ and V _ _ _ _ _ _ are the two main *micro-organisms* which can cause disease.

b) Complete the table below, by putting the letters A-E in the appropriate column.

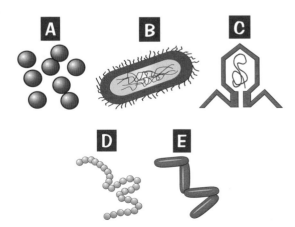

Bacteria	Viruses

c) Which micro-organisms invade living cells ?

....

Questions on Health

Q7 a) *There are millions of <u>bacteria</u> everywhere - in your skin, air, water and soil. Some are important and do useful jobs (e.g. production of yoghurt), but others cause disease.* List three ways in which bacteria can enter the body.

....

....

b) Explain why it is important to cover your mouth or nose when you cough or sneeze.

....

....

....

c) When bacteria enter our body and start to multiply, what do we say we have?

....

d) *Bacteria can get into drinking water and make you ill when you drink it.*

Which disease can be spread in this way?

....

e) Why should we not eat food which is undercooked?

....

....

....

Q8   Put a tick or cross in the box at the end of each statement to indicate whether it is correct.

✓ ✗

A *Addict* – a person who needs a drug to feel normal. ☐

B *Alcoholic* – a person who only drinks alcohol at breakfast. ☐

C Solvents do not damage the brain. ☐

D The side-effects of taking drugs can permanently damage your health. ☐

E A small amount of alcohol has no effect at all on the body. ☐

F Viruses are larger than bacteria. ☐

G A sneeze can travel as fast as a hurricane. ☐

H Micro-organisms can be seen with the naked eye. ☐

Questions on Fighting Disease

Q1 Fill in the gaps. All the words you need are in the word box, but so are some you don't.

| immune   disease   red   medicines   natural defences   germs |
| immunisation   skin   white blood cells   antibodies   health |

The body has its own _____ _____ against disease but it can be

helped by _____ and _____. The main armies of

defence of the body are _____ and _____ _____

_____ which are part of the body's _____ system.

Q2 Complete the sentences by ringing the correct word to show how a cut in the skin is _sealed_ and the entry of bacteria is _prevented_.

When the skin is cut, (dirt/bacteria) can enter and cause disease, so (platelets/healthy cells) in the blood seal the wound. During this process (red/white) blood cells come to the site of damage and either (eat/repel) the bacteria or produce (antibodies/safe germs) to fight them.

Q3 a) What are the three ways that white blood cells fight microbes?

....

....

....

b) Complete the following sentence.

Once you have had a disease the **a** _ _ _ _ _ _ _ _ _ are produced much

quicker the next time and your body has some **i** _ _ _ _ _ _ _ _ .

Q4 a) Which _process (which is a good way to help the body defend against disease)_ does the diagram A show?

....

b) What is placed _into the body_ during this process?

....

A

c) What is the _job_ of the substance named in **b)**?

....

....

d) What is the name of the _liquid_ which can protect you if you are given it before you have the disease?

— Arm

....

e) Which group of medical chemicals _kill bacteria_ and are very useful in treating diseases _(but are not antibodies)_?

....

PLANTS AS ORGANISMS

Questions on Plant Nutrition

Q1   *Plants make sugars in their leaves using <u>carbon dioxide</u>, <u>water</u> and <u>energy</u> from sunlight.*

   a) What name do we give to the process that plants use to make their own food?

....

   b) Some insect pests eat plant leaves. What could happen to a plant infested by these insects?

....

   The roots of some plants go far down into the soil, others spread just under the surface.

   c) Name three functions (jobs) of the roots?

....

....

....

   d) Some insect pests eat plant roots. What could happen to a plant infested by these insects?

....

Q2   *Liz visited a garden centre. There were lots of bottles of <u>fertiliser</u> on display with a big sign
saying "Feed your tomato plants! New Growall is all the food your plants need — buy it
now!" Liz wasn't happy with the sign, and thought it wasn't accurate.*
Why was she unhappy — what is wrong with the idea that a fertiliser feeds your plants with
all the food they need?

....

....

....

Q3   *If you study a root using a microscope, you see
tiny <u>root hair cells</u> like the one in the picture.*

What substances are absorbed through the
surface of the root hair cells and why do roots
have root hairs and not just smooth surfaces?

....

....

....

....

Questions on Plant Nutrition

Q4 *Scientists at the Pudsey Plant Research Centre wanted to find out what plants need to grow properly. They set up four beakers of water and put some small water plants in each. They then added some minerals to the beakers, and recorded the growth of the plants over the next few days. Their results are shown in the table below.*

Beaker	Minerals	Appearance of plants
A	nitrate, phosphate, potassium	lots of healthy green leaves
B	nitrate and phosphate	leaves are yellow with dead spots
C	nitrate and potassium	leaves turning purple, roots not growing very well
D	phosphate and potassium	yellow leaves with weak stems

a) Which *mineral* is missing from beaker B compared to beaker A? What happens to plants if this mineral is missing? ....

b) Which *mineral* is needed for roots to grow properly? Explain how you know this.

....

....

c) What happens to plants if *nitrate* is missing? ....

....

d) What would happen if you tried to grow plants in *pure water* with no minerals?

....

e) *Nitrates provide nitrogen and phosphates provide phosphorus.*
Explain why i) nitrogen and ii) phosphorus are important for plant growth.

i) ....

ii) ....

Q5 *This is a list of the features of many leaves:*
A) *They are flat and wide;*
B) *They are thin;*
C) *They have lots of veins;*
D) *They have little holes (stomata) in the lower surface.*
Explain how each feature lets the leaf make food for the plant efficiently.

A) ....

B) ....

C) ....

D) ....

44

Questions on Photosynthesis

Q1 *In an experiment with two plants, one was put on the <u>windowsill</u>, and the other was shut in a <u>dark cupboard</u>. Both were watered regularly. After three days, the plant in the cupboard was taken out and compared with the other one. The plant from the windowsill looked green and healthy, but the other looked pale and some of its leaves had fallen off.*

    a) How do we know that <u>lack of water</u> was not to blame for the differences between the plants?

....

....

    b) *It was suggested that the plant in the cupboard was not as healthy as the one on the windowsill in the first place.* What could you do to the experiment to show that this was not the cause of the difference?

....

....

    c) Give a reason for the difference between the two plants after three days.

....

    Two more plants were put on the windowsill. One was given water but the other one wasn't.

    d) What do you expect to happen to the plant without water? ....

....

    e) What do these two experiments tell you about plants — what things do they need to grow?

....

....

Q2 *Cress seeds were sprinkled in two dishes lined with kitchen roll. The same amount of water was added to each dish to make the paper wet. After planting, the seeds were kept in different conditions. The pictures show how they grew.*
Explain what <u>conditions</u> each dish might have been put in.

Dish A   Dish B

....

....

....

Section Five — Plants as Organisms

Questions on Photosynthesis

Q3 A green leaf was boiled in water to soften it, and then boiled in ethanol. It was washed with water and some brown iodine solution was dropped onto it. The extra iodine solution was washed away.

a) The ethanol in the experiment turned green and the leaf went white. Why did this happen?

....

b) When the iodine was added to the leaf, it turned blue-black. What does this mean?

....

A plant with green leaves was put in the dark for two days, then a leaf was tested with iodine.

c) What result would you expect? Why would you expect this to happen?

....

....

Q4 The diagram to the right shows an experiment to study _photosynthesis_ in pond weed. Bubbles made by the plant when a lamp was shone on it were collected in the test-tube. A glowing splint relit when put into the test-tube.

What _gas_ is produced during photosynthesis? How do you know this?

Gas / Test-tube / Water / Beaker / Pond weed / Funnel / Plasticine

....

....

....

Q5 _Soda lime absorbs carbon dioxide._ A plant sealed in a container with a dish of soda lime begins to turn yellow and dies, even if it gets lots of light, water and minerals.

What does this tell you about _photosynthesis?_

....

....

....

....

46

Questions on Photosynthesis

Q6   *The list below shows substances involved in photosynthesis:*

   oxygen   carbon dioxide   water   chlorophyll   glucose

   a) Which *gas* goes into the leaf for photosynthesis, and which gas comes out of the leaf?

   ....

   b) What colour is *chlorophyll,* and what does it do? ....

   ....

   c) Is water needed for *photosynthesis,* or is it made by photosynthesis?

   ....

   d) What substances are *made* by photosynthesis? ....

   e) Complete this *word equation* for photosynthesis using the words at the top of the page:

.... **+** .... $\xrightarrow{\text{light}}$ **Glucose +** ....

   f) Light is shown in the equation. *Why* is light needed for photosynthesis?

   ....

   ....

Q7   Does photosynthesis happen at *night?* Explain your answer.

   ....

   ....

Q8   *The picture below shows a tree growing in a field. The Sun is shining, so photosynthesis is taking place rapidly in the leaves.*

   a) What substance is *taken in* from the air by the tree? ....

   b) What substance is *given out* into the air by the tree? ....

   c) What substance needed for *photosynthesis* does the tree take
   from the soil?

   ....

   ....

Questions on Photosynthesis

Q9 Explain why *photosynthesis* is important to ourselves and other animals.

....

....

....

Q10 *Complete* the photosynthesis crossword:

Across

3) Sugars are stored as this (6)
5) and **6)** down — gas needed
    for photosynthesis (6,7)
10) How plants make food (14)
11) Food is made here (4)
13) Chlorophyll looks like this (5)

Down

1) Plants can't photosynthesise in this (4)
2) We need it — plants make it in the light (6)
3) Roots get water from here (4)
4) Pigment that absorbs light (11)
6) see 5) across
7) Energy needed to make sugars (5)
8) Liquid needed for photosynthesis (5)
9) Test for starch with this solution (6)
12) Carbon dioxide comes from here (3)

Questions on Plant Growth

Q1   Complete these sentences about *plant growth*, by ringing the correct words from the pairs.

"Roots grow (**towards** / **away from**) the light, and (**with** / **against**) gravity."

"Shoots grow (**towards** / **away from**) the light, and (**towards** / **away from**) gravity."

Q2   Match the *beginning* of each sentence to the correct *ending* with an arrow:

Beginnings ⟶ Endings

Beginnings	Endings
nitrogen is needed for	glucose
phosphorus is needed for	healthy green leaves
photosynthesis is needed for	photosynthesis
potassium is needed for	glucose and oxygen production
starch is made from	strong stems and green leaves
water and carbon dioxide are needed for	healthy root growth

Q3   *Farmer Palmer wanted to find the* <u>best conditions</u> *to grow his tomato plants. In the first experiment, the rate of photosynthesis was measured at different levels of light intensity. His results are shown on the graph on the right.*

a)   Why should he be interested in the rate of photosynthesis when he wanted to find out the *growth* of his plants?

....

....

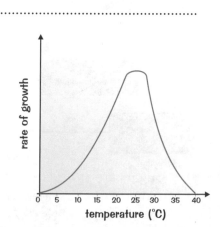

b)   What is the light intensity where the rate of photosynthesis reaches its maximum? Should Farmer Palmer use 10 units of light intensity to try to get his plants to grow faster?

....

In the next experiment, the tomato plants were grown at <u>different temperatures</u>. *The second graph on the right shows the results.*

c)   At what temperatures do the plants stop growing?

....

d)   What temperature is needed to get the plants to

grow at their fastest rate?   ....

e)   Heating and lighting cost money. Explain what Farmer Palmer should do to get his tomato plants to grow very quickly but without wasting money. *(Clue: Why do you think tomatoes are often grown in greenhouses instead of outside?)*

....

....

Questions on Plant Reproduction

Taken out
of the curriculum
but still important

Q1 Look at the diagram of a *flowering plant*.

a) Match the following parts to the labels W, X, Y and Z:

stem .... / roots .... / flower .... / leaf ....

b) Which part of the plant, W, X, Y or Z:

– absorbs water and minerals? ....

– absorbs light for photosynthesis? ....

– anchors the plant? ....

– contains the reproductive organs? ....

– makes food for the plant? ....

– supports the plant? ....

c) What are the functions (jobs) of the roots, stem, leaves, and flowers?

Roots: ....

Stem: ....

Leaves: ....

Flowers: ....

Q2 Complete this sentence about sexual reproduction in plants, by ringing the correct words:
The (**male** / **female**) sex cell is the pollen, and the (**male** / **female**) sex cell is the (**ovule** / **ovum**).

Q3 *The diagram opposite is a cut-away diagram of a flower.*

a) Add labels and labelling lines to the *anther* and the *filament* parts of the Stamen (this is the male part of the flower — remember it as sta*men*). What is the job of the filament? What is the job of the anther?

....

....

....

b) Add labels and labelling lines to the *stigma*, the *style* and the *ovary*. What part of the flower do these three parts make? ....

c) What do you expect to find in the ovary? ....

d) Add labels and labelling lines to the *sepals* and the *petals*.

SECTION FIVE — PLANTS AS ORGANISMS

Questions on Plant Reproduction

Taken out
of the curriculum
but still important

Q4 a) What is the main difference in appearance between the sepals and the petals?

....

b) What is the function of the sepals? ....

c) What is the function of the petals? ....

Q5 Complete the sentences, by joining a beginning with an ending with an arrow:

Beginnings

the female sex cell in plants is called

the female sex organ in plants is called

the female sex organ is made up from

the male sex cell in plants is called

the male sex organ in plants is called

the male sex organ is made up from

Endings

the filament and anther

the stigma, style and ovary

the carpel

the stamen

the pollen

the ovule

Q6 Below are the names of plants. Three are pollinated by insects, and three are pollinated by the wind. Decide which are which and fill in the table below appropriately.

insect-pollinated	wind-pollinated

buttercup   stinging nettle

grass   sunflower

dandelion

willow tree

Q7 Have a go at the flower wordsearch.
The words to find are:

anther, filament, ovary, ovule,
pollen, stigma, style.

There are two other words in the grid to do with flowers — can you find them both?
Here's a clue..

S _ _ _ _ N

C _ _ _ _ L

W	P	A	O	V	U	L	E	R	A
C	Z	N	T	E	B	Z	E	M	O
A	E	T	N	I	H	E	G	V	G
R	Y	H	E	U	U	I	I	D	S
P	R	E	M	Z	T	K	E	X	P
E	A	R	A	S	Q	X	A	S	O
L	V	F	L	D	F	N	T	S	L
N	O	K	I	C	O	Y	O	L	L
H	P	A	F	Q	L	D	N	P	E
S	T	A	M	E	N	Y	Y	B	N

Questions on Plant Reproduction

Q8 *The pictures on the right show two flowers cut away. One is a wind-pollinated flower, the other is an insect-pollinated flower.*

A   **B**

a) What does *pollination* mean?

....

....

b) Which picture shows the *wind-pollinated flower?* Explain how the flower is adapted to

pollination by the wind. ....

....

c) Which picture shows the *insect-pollinated flower?* Explain how the flower is adapted to

pollination by insects. ....

....

d) Pollen from wind-pollinated flowers is often much lighter and smaller than the pollen from insect-pollinated flowers. Why do you think there is this difference between them?

....

....

Q9 Read the information below, then answer the questions.

> *Cross-pollination* is when the pollen of a flower lands on the stigma of another flower.
> *Self-pollination* is when the pollen of a flower lands on the stigma of the same flower.
> *Cross-pollination allows more variety between plants, often producing better quality seeds, and many plants have adaptations to make cross-pollination more likely than self-pollination.*

a) What is the difference between self-pollination and cross-pollination?

....

....

b) The statements below give two adaptations. For each adaptation, suggest why it should make cross-pollination more likely than self-pollination.
— some plants only have male flowers, and others only have female flowers.

....

....

— the stamens and carpels mature at different times.

....

....

SECTION FIVE — PLANTS AS ORGANISMS

Questions on Fertilisation and Seed Formation

Q1a) When a pollen grain lands on a stigma, a *pollen tube* grows down to the ovary and then into it. What is the name of the part of the flower that the pollen tube grows through?

....

b) The nucleus from the pollen grain passes through the pollen tube, meets the female sex cell, and joins with it. When a male sex cell joins with a female sex cell, what is this called?

....

c) The *fertilised ovule* grows into a seed. In which part of the flower does this happen?

....

Taken o
of the curriculum
but still import

d) Once the seeds have developed enough, they are dispersed from the parent plant. What does *dispersed* mean? ....

....

e) *Some of the dispersed seeds will begin to grow into a new plant if the conditions are right.* What name is given to the process of a *seed* starting to grow into a *seedling*?

....

Q2 The processes below are all to do with reproduction by flowering plants. Write them down in the correct order, starting with "release of pollen" and ending with "growth of seedling".

| Dispersal | Fertilisation | Germination | Pollination |

| Growth of seedling | Growth of pollen tube | Release of pollen | Seed production |

Release of Pollen → ....

....

....

....

....

Fertilisation and Seed Formation

Taken out
of the curriculum
but still important

Q3 *Plants have developed various methods to carry their seeds far from the parent plant. Some plants, such as peas and lupins, are able to flick the seeds away from them. As with the transfer of pollen in pollination, plants can spread their seeds using the wind or animals.*

a) The pictures show seeds from *dandelions* and *sycamore trees*. These plants rely on the wind to spread their seeds. For each seed, use the picture to explain how it is adapted to carry it far away from the parent.

Dandelion   Sycamore

....

....

....

....

In many plants, the ovary develops into a fleshy fruit that contains the seeds. Fruits contain sugars and often have bright colours.

Bright red skin

Little hooks like "velcro"

Tomato   Burdock

b) What is the advantage to an *animal* of eating a fruit?

....

....

c) What is the advantage to a *plant* of having its fruits eaten by animals?

....

....

d) The pictures show fruits from tomatoes and burdock. The plants rely on animals to spread their seeds. For each fruit, use the information in the picture to explain how it is adapted to carry the seeds far away from the parent.

....

....

....

....

e) Name a fruit eaten by animals. Suggest why it is attractive to animals.

....

....

Questions on The Carbon Cycle

Q1   In your answers to the questions below, choose from the following gases:

nitrogen   oxygen   argon   carbon dioxide

a) Which gas in the air is needed for wood to burn?

....

b) When wood burns, water vapour is made. What else is made?

....

c) Use your answers to parts **(a)** and **(b)** to complete this *word equation* for *burning:*

wood + ... → water + ...

d) To stay alive we need to *respire*. Which gas in the air do we need to breathe in to stay

alive? ....

When we breathe out, our breath contains less of this gas, but a lot more of another gas.

Which other gas? ....

e) Use your answers to part (d) to complete this *word equation* for *respiration:*

glucose + ... → water + ...

f) Look at your answers to parts (c) and (e). What do you notice about them?

....

....

g) The word equation for photosynthesis is:

carbon dioxide + water   → (Sun's energy)   glucose + oxygen.

What do you notice about burning, respiration and photosynthesis?

....

....

....

....

Questions on The Carbon Cycle

Q2 We can put burning, respiration and photosynthesis together to make the *carbon cycle*.
The diagram below shows part of the carbon cycle.
Fill in the names for processes 1, 2 and 3.

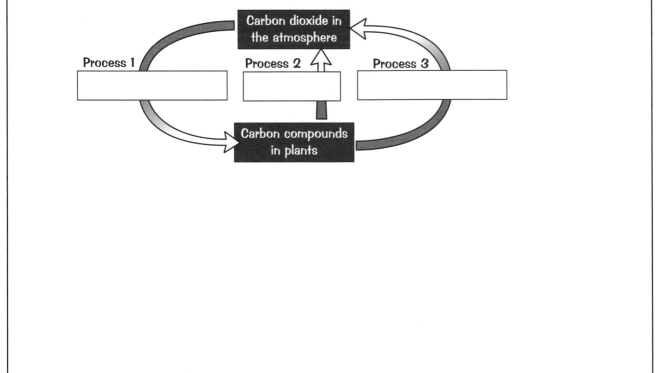

Q3a) *Carbon compounds* such as glucose can get into animals, and carbon compounds in these

animals can get into other animals. How does this happen? ....

....

b) Add labelled arrows and boxes to your diagram from question 2 to show carbon
compounds getting into animals.

c) What happens to the carbon compounds in animals that are not needed?

....

d) Draw another labelled arrow to show what happens to these wastes.

Q4 Look at the following list. Which of these things *respire?*

bacterium,   bird,   dandelion,   dead donkey,   dog,   fish,   frog,
human,   seaweed,   snake,   soil,   wooden table

....

....

Q5 Bacteria can feed on dead animals, plants and animal wastes. They respire as they do this.
Add a final labelled arrow to your diagram to complete your carbon cycle.

56

Questions on The Nitrogen Cycle

Q1 The sentences below explain all about _nitrogen fixation_ (the change of nitrogen gas into a more reactive form, e.g. nitrates), but they are all in the wrong order. Read through them all, then answer the questions.

1) This acid makes nitrates in the soil.	3) The energy from lightning gets nitrogen to react with oxygen.	6) It takes a lot of enery to get nitrogen to react with oxygen.
2) Nitrogen is a very unreactive gas.	4) Nitrogen oxides are made when nitrogen and oxygen react.	7) When nitrogen oxides dissolve in rainwater, they make an acid.
	5) Plants can use nitrates to make proteins.	

a) Explain how you know that a lot of energy is needed to get nitrogen and oxygen to react.

....

....

b) What is made when oxygen and nitrogen react together? ....

c) Explain how the substance in your answer to part (b) allows plants to make proteins.

....

....

d) Write down the sentences 1 – 7 in the correct order, and use them to help you explain how nitrogen fixation works.

....

....

....

....

....

....

....

....

....

....

....

....

Questions on The Nitrogen Cycle

Q2 *There are bacteria in the soil called <u>denitrifying bacteria</u>. They convert nitrates in the soil back into nitrogen gas. The diagram below shows how nitrogen in the air can be converted into nitrates in the soil, and then back to nitrogen again.*

a) Fill in the missing labels in the diagram below.

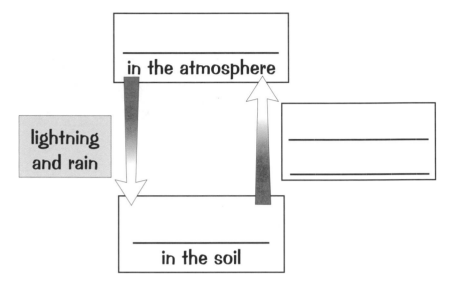

b) This diagram is part of the *<u>nitrogen cycle</u>*. Why do you think it is called a *cycle?*

....

Q3 *When animals eat plants, the <u>protein</u> in the plants is used to make protein in the animals.*

a) What substance do plants need from the soil to make proteins? ....

b) Give the names of two tissues or parts of an animal that are made of protein.

....

c) Add labelled arrows and boxes to your nitrogen cycle to show how the substance in the soil gets into animal proteins.

Q4 When animals and plants die, *<u>decay bacteria</u>* break the proteins down into nitrates in the soil. Add labelled arrows and boxes to your nitrogen cycle to show how proteins in plants and animals end up as nitrates in the soil.

Q5 Use your completed nitrogen cycle to answer these questions:

a) What processes produce nitrates in the soil? ....

b) What processes take nitrates out of the soil? ....

c) What jobs do the different bacteria do in the nitrogen cycle?

....

....

....

SECTION FIVE — PLANTS AS ORGANISMS

Questions on Variation

Q1   *The tally chart below shows the eye colour of the children in a class at school. Eye colour is an example of <u>discontinuous variation</u> because there are a limited number of distinct options.*

Eye Colour	Brown	Blue	Green	Hazel
Tally of Students	̶H̶H̶ IIII	̶H̶H̶ ̶H̶H̶ II	̶H̶H̶	̶H̶H̶ I

a) <u>*Complete*</u> the table on the right with the numbers of children with each eye colour.

b) On the graph paper below, draw a *bar chart* of number of children against eye colour. The vertical (side) axis should be the number of children (1 large square per child works well). The horizontal (bottom) axis should be divided into four equal parts, one for each eye colour. For each eye colour, plot the number of children as a bar on the chart. Make sure you label each axis with the headings from your table, and give your graph a title.

Colour of eyes	Number of children
Brown	
Blue	
Green	
Hazel	

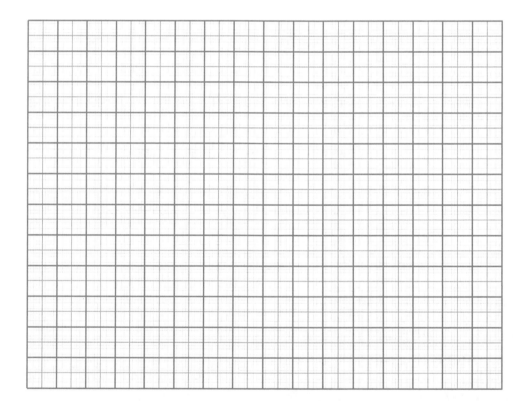

c) How many children altogether were included in the results? What percentage of the children had green eyes? Make sure you show your working out.

....

....

Questions on Variation

Q2 *The heights of the girls in two Year 7 classes were measured. The results are shown on the right. You are going to draw a graph to show these results.*

Height (cm)					
152	148	143	147	160	168
156	154	146	141	151	153
159	158	155	157	159	146
152	154	160	164	144	136
153	150	148	149	163	158

Height range (cm)	Number of girls
135-139	
140-144	
145-149	
150-154	
155-159	
160-164	
165-169	

a) Carefully work your way through the recorded heights, filling in the number of girls at each height range in the tally chart on the left. There are 30 girls altogether, so check that your tally count adds up to 30. If it doesn't, you have gone wrong somewhere.

b) On the graph paper below, draw a *bar chart* of the results. The vertical (side) axis should be the number of girls (1 large square per girl works well). The horizontal (bottom) axis should be divided into seven equal parts, one for each height range. Plot each number of girls from your tally chart as a bar. Make sure you label each axis and give your graph a title.

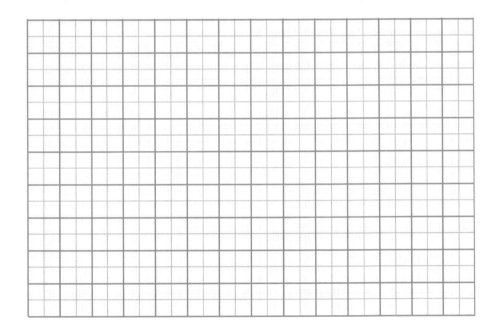

c) How tall would a girl have to be to be among the tallest five girls? How tall would she have to be to be among the shortest ten girls?

Amongst Tallest ....   Amongst Shortest ....

d) *Although we measured the girls' heights to the nearest centimetre, and plotted their heights in ranges of 5cm, if we had a very precise ruler we could measure to tiny fractions of a centimetre. This is continuous variation because, for example, a girl could be any height between 150cm and 151cm, not just 150cm or 151cm. Give two more examples of continuous variation in people.*

....

Questions on Environmental & Inherited Variation

Q1 *Animals and plants do not all look the same, they vary. Some of this <u>variation</u> is <u>inherited</u> from their parents, and some is caused by the <u>environment</u> (where a plant grows, how you are brought up and what you eat, for example).*

a) Compare the appearance of a <u>*tree*</u> with <u>*yourself*</u>. Give four ways in which you and the tree are different (hopefully there are plenty). Can you think of any ways in which your appearance is the same?

....

....

....

b) Compare the appearance of a <u>*chimpanzee*</u> with <u>*yourself*</u>. Give three ways in which you and the chimpanzee are different, and three ways in which you are similar.

....

....

....

c) <u>*Compare*</u> the appearance of one of your friends or family with yourself. Give three ways in which you are different from this person, and three ways in which you are similar.

....

....

....

d) Look back at your answers to parts a), b) and c). For each difference between you and the tree, chimpanzee or other person, write down whether you think the difference is <u>*inherited*</u> or due to the <u>*environment*</u>. Parts a) and b) should be fairly easy, but part c) might be harder – you might have difficulties deciding if a difference is due to environmental variation, inherited variation, or both. If you think it is due to both, say so and explain why.

....

....

....

....

....

....

SECTION SIX — VARIATION

Questions on Environmental & Inherited Variation

Q2 *Spider plants* are houseplants that produce lots of baby spider plants on *runners* from the parent plant (see the picture on the right). Every baby spider plant inherits the same information from the parent. Linda's spider plant has lots of baby spider plants. She plants several of them in separate pots, and lets them grow ready to sell at the school fair. Linda expected that all the new plants would grow the same because they came from the same parent plant, but some are bushier or taller than others.

Baby Spider plants on runners from parent plant

Spider Plant

Name four *environmental factors* that could affect the growth of the plants. For each factor, explain what effect it would have on the growth of the plants.

1) ....
....

2) ....
....

3) ....
....

4) ....
....

Q3 *Identical twins* have exactly the same genes as each other. So they may both have brown eyes as this is an inherited feature. But one twin could weigh more than the other — this is an environmental feature because this twin might eat more than the other.

The list below gives some features of an old man called Bob. Decide which of Bob's features have been inherited from his parents, and which are due to his environment.

   1) dark brown hair   2) blood group is O negative   3) short hair with a parting
   4) scar under one eye   5) first name is Bob   6) speaks English   7) yellow fingers

....
....
....
....
....

Questions on Inheritance and Selective Breeding

Q1 Read this example of *selective breeding*, then answer the questions below.

> Panjit Jones, a budgerigar fancier, was having his birds beaten in shows because they were too small. He decided to change his <u>breeding program</u> to produce larger budgies. Some of his birds were bigger than the rest, so Panjit only allowed these birds to breed. When the baby birds had grown up, the smallest were sold to a pet shop, and the largest were allowed to breed. Panjit found that he had to keep doing this for several years until most of the birds he bred were large enough to win prizes at shows.

a) What did Panjit do to make sure that he was selecting for this feature?

....

....

....

b) Suggest why it took Panjit several years to produce a prize-winning flock.

....

....

....

c) Why is Panjit's breeding programme an example of *selective breeding?*

....

....

....

d) Panjit's birds did not all win prizes, even if they were large. Many of them did not have nice enough beaks to impress the judges. Describe how Panjit should change his breeding programme to produce large birds with lovely beaks.

....

....

....

....

Questions on Inheritance and Selective Breeding

Q2 *Dogs are descended from wolves.*
Pedigree dogs always produce puppies that show the features of the breed. Look at the pictures of the wolf, the golden retriever and the bulldog.

Golden Retriever

Bulldog

Wolf

a) What features have been selected to produce pedigree golden retrievers from wolves?

....

....

....

b) What features have been selected to produce pedigree bulldogs from wolves?

....

....

c) Suggest two problems you might find if you tried to breed bulldogs from pedigree golden retrievers.

....

....

....

Q3 *Farmers often want to improve their crops or livestock.*
Study the pictures below. They show original "*wild type*" plant or animal, and the crop and livestock produced from them by *selective breeding*. For each one, write down which features have been selected for breeding, and suggest one other desirable feature not shown in the pictures.

Wild Wheat   **Modern Wheat**   **Wild Boar**   **Modern Pig**

....

....

....

....

Questions on Classification of Plants & Animals

Q1 Give three differences between *plants* and *animals*.

....

....

....

Q2 *Mammals* and *birds* are two groups of animals that have backbones.

a) What do we call animals with *backbones*?

....

b) Give three examples of a mammal, and three examples of a bird.

....

....

....

c) Give three differences between a mammal and a bird.

....

....

d) Give three features that mammals and birds have in common.

....

....

e) *Fish are another group of animals with backbones.*
Apart from living in water, give three differences between fish, and mammals and birds.

....

....

....

f) *Reptiles* and *amphibians* are two more groups of animals with backbones.
Give two examples of a reptile, and two examples of an amphibian. How could you tell a reptile from an amphibian?

....

....

....

Questions on Classification of Plants & Animals

Q3 Animals without backbones are called <u>invertebrates</u>. Some have legs, others do not. Invertebrates with legs are called <u>arthropods</u>. There are four main groups.

a) Use the information below to decide which group each animal in the picture belongs to.

....

....

Group	Features
Arachnids (spiders)	Hard body divided into two main parts, eight legs
Crustaceans	Hard body divided into lots of segments, many legs
Insects	Hard body divided into three main parts, six legs, may have wings
Myriapods	Hard body divided into lots of segments, very many legs

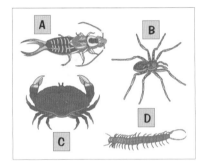

b) Give four features that the groups of organisms in the table have in common.

....

....

....

....

c) Give two ways to tell a wingless insect from a spider. ....

....

d) What is an <u>arthropod?</u> ....

....

Q4 There are many invertebrate groups without legs. A <u>coelenterate</u> has a sack-like body with tentacles; <u>molluscs</u> have soft, slimy bodies, and may have a shell; <u>segmented worms</u> have soft, wet, long bodies divided into rings; <u>flatworms</u> and <u>roundworms</u> are long and thin but are not divided into rings.
The <u>word search</u> on the right contains eight words from the paragraph above. Can you find them all?

M _ _ _ _ _ _ , F _ _ _ _ _ _ _ _ ,

R _ _ _ _ _ _ _ _ _ _ , S _ _ _ _ _ ,

C _ _ _ _ _ _ _ _ _ _ _ ,

I _ _ _ _ _ _ _ _ _ _ _ ,

S _ _ _ _ _ _ _ _ , S _ _ _ _ ,

```
E  M  O  L  L  U  S  C  Y  S  I  E
R  T  Z  B  C  D  Y  G  H  R  T  L
O  C  A  Q  E  C  C  E  E  A  O  S
U  J  D  R  W  D  L  V  R  K  E  E
N  Y  G  S  E  L  M  B  A  G  Q  A
D  M  I  J  X  T  E  I  M  I  C  E
W  I  Q  L  V  T  N  E  Z  N  B  I
O  L  P  N  R  R  N  E  Z  L  T  X
R  S  P  E  T  T  V  B  L  H  M  A
M  J  V  Z  E  T  O  D  S  E  G  K
Q  N  J  D  R  B  L  A  R  Q  O  E
I  M  R  O  W  T  A  L  F  T  Z  C
```

66

Questions on Keys

Taken out
of the curriculum
but still important

Q1 This *key* can be used to name these shapes:

A B C D

1) Does it have three sides?	Yes	triangle	No	go to question 2
2) Does it have five sides?	Yes	pentagon	No	go to question 3
3) Are the sides all the same?	Yes	square	No	rectangle

Use this key to identify the four shapes above.

....

Now alter the key so that it will also let you identify a circle and
an ellipse (see box to the right).

circle

ellipse

....

....

....

....

Q2 The pictures on the right show some
common laboratory apparatus.

beaker   test tube

measuring
cylinder

conical flask

round-bottomed flask

a) Work out your own key to tell them apart.

....

....

....

....

....

b) Explain how your key would be useful to someone who didn't know laboratory equipment.

....

....

SECTION SEVEN — ORGANISMS IN THEIR ENVIRONMENT

Questions on Keys

Taken out
of the curriculum
but still important

Q3 The pictures show some *insects*. Use the key to identify each insect. Put your answers in a table below. You need to be able to recognise the *abdomen* (with the *tail* — which is the section on the left of the insects below) the *head* (here on the right), and the *thorax* (which is the section with the legs attached).

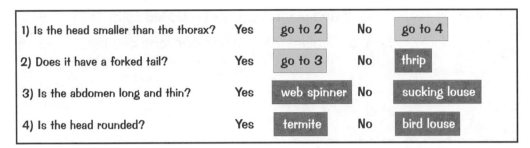

1) Is the head smaller than the thorax?	Yes	go to 2	No	go to 4
2) Does it have a forked tail?	Yes	go to 3	No	thrip
3) Is the abdomen long and thin?	Yes	web spinner	No	sucking louse
4) Is the head rounded?	Yes	termite	No	bird louse

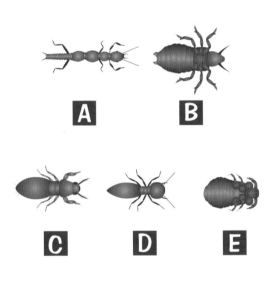

A B C D E

label	name
A	

Q4 Think of some people, animals, plants, objects or places that you might want to classify. Work out a key to identify them below. A good key will ask one less question than the number of objects. Does yours?

....

....

....

....

....

....

....

....

68

Questions on Adaptation

Q1 Complete these sentences by circling the correct words in the brackets:

The place where something lives is called its (**habitat** / **environment**).

The conditions in a habitat are the (**environment** / **situation**).

Over millions of years, animals and plants become (**adapted** / **similar**) to their environment.

Q2 a) The pictures (below right) show a plant that lives on land, and one that lives in the sea (bladder wrack). What features do they have in common?

....

....

....

b) How do these features allow the plant to be adapted to its environment?

....

....

....

....

Plant that lives on land   Plant that lives in the sea

c) Land plants have sturdy stems that allow them to stay upright. Why should the plant need

to stay upright? ....

....

d) If bladder wrack is uncovered by the tide, it flops onto the ground. Why does this happen?

....

....

....

e) It is called bladder wrack because of the little air bladders on its fronds. What are these for? – what do you think will happen when the tide comes in and the bladder wrack gets covered by water?

....

....

....

....

SECTION SEVEN — ORGANISMS IN THEIR ENVIRONMENT

Questions on Adaptation

Q3 *In the desert, it sometimes doesn't rain for years, although there can be a lot of water when it does rain. There can be very strong winds that whip up the sand and cause it to drift. Though the days are very hot, the nights are cold, and in the morning there is often dew on the ground. Some plants in the desert have shallow roots that spread just below the surface, whereas others have very long roots that reach deep underground.*

a) Explain how the two different types of root are *adapted* to obtaining water in the desert. Are there any other *advantages* to having roots like these? Are there any *disadvantages?*

....

....

....

b) The list below shows some other *features* of desert plants. Suggest how they help the plants to be adapted to life in the desert.
      1) The seeds can lie dormant in the soil for years until the rain comes.
      2) Succulent plants store water in their leaves, stems, and roots.
      3) They usually have small leaves, or modified leaves which form thorns.

1) ....

....

2) ....

....

3) ....

....

c) How are camels *adapted* to life in the desert? Think of as many adaptations as you can and, for each one, explain how it helps the camel to live in the desert.

....

....

....

....

....

....

....

....

Questions on Food Chains and Food Webs

Q1   Draw arrows to match the *words* to the *meanings*.

carnivores   animals that can eat both plants and animals

omnivores   animals that eat plants

herbivores   animals that eat other animals

consumers   organisms that can make their own food

producers   organisms that rely on other organisms for their food

Q2   In the food chain below, what do the arrows mean? ....

tiny plants → squid → whale

Write down the name of the *herbivore*, the *carnivore*, and the *producer*. Explain how you

know this. ....

....

....

Q3   Food chains always begin with a certain type of living thing. What type of living thing is this? Write down two examples of this type of living thing. Why do they start off food chains?

....

....

Q4   The names below are all words to do with food chains, but with the letters muddled up. Unscramble the letters to find out what the words are and then find them in the word search:

Vince Roar, Mrs Oncue, Dina Choof, Ron Movie, Dr Prouce, Rover Hibe.

....

....

....

....

....

....

....

E	P	C	O	N	S	U	M	E	R
R	R	F	O	I	D	C	H	A	O
O	E	O	O	A	E	R	B	M	I
V	C	O	M	H	I	V	N	C	A
I	U	D	A	C	H	I	N	G	R
B	D	C	E	D	V	O	R	E	S
R	O	H	S	O	K	I	Z	X	L
E	R	A	R	O	A	R	N	I	V
H	P	E	R	F	V	I	B	R	A
X	E	R	O	V	I	N	R	A	C

Questions on Food Chains and Food Webs

Q5 *Look at the woodland __food web__.*

a) Name the carnivores. Which one is not a top

carnivore? ....

b) Write down all the food chains that start with the
blackberry and end with the hawk.

....

....

....

c) Write down all the food chains that end with the owl.

....

....

d) Explain what might happen to the number of voles and rabbits if the amount of grass
increased.

....

....

e) Explain what might happen to the number of owls if the amount of grass increased.

....

....

f) Explain what might happen to the number of blue tits if the hawk dies.

....

....

g) Explain what might happen to the number of aphids if the hawk dies.

....

....

Q6 Decide whether each of the following sentences is true (**T**) or false (**F**) and then tick the
appropriate box.

	T	F
"Primary consumers are always herbivores."	☐	☐
"Carnivores are always secondary consumers."	☐	☐
"In a food web, arrows can point in any direction."	☐	☐
"Top carnivores are always very large".	☐	☐

SECTION SEVEN — ORGANISMS IN THEIR ENVIRONMENT

Questions on Number Pyramids

Q1 *A pyramid of numbers is shown on the right.*

    a) Label the *primary consumer,* the *secondary consumer* and the *producer*.

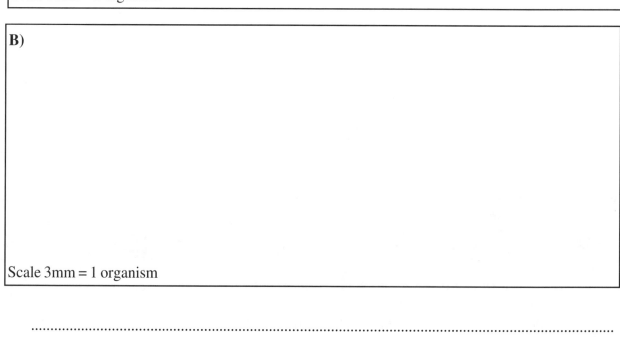

Fox (1)

Rabbit (10)

Grass (1 million)

    b) What information do the widths of the bars give us?

....

Q2 Here are two *food chains* with the numbers of each organism:

    A)   grass (50) → vole (10) → owl (1)

    B)   oak tree (1) → caterpillar (50) → blue tit (10)

Draw the pyramids of numbers for these food chains. Draw them to scale, and label the bars with the name and number of each organism. One of the two pyramids doesn't look very pyramid-shaped. Explain why it looks like it does.

A)

Scale 3mm = 1 organism

B)

Scale 3mm = 1 organism

....

....

Questions on Number Pyramids

Q3   The following diagrams show four different pyramids of numbers.

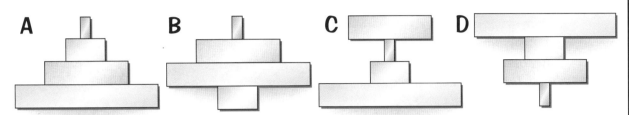

Match these food chains to the pyramids above, and explain why you think they match.

a) blackberry → vole → fox → flea is the food chain represented by pyramid ....

....

....

b) grass → snail → bird → stoat is the food chain represented by pyramid ....

....

....

c) oak tree → caterpillars → bird → flea is the food chain represented by pyramid ....

....

....

d) rose bush → aphid → ladybird → bird is the food chain represented by pyramid ....

....

....

Q4 a) In which *direction* does energy flow in a food chain? In which direction does it go in a pyramid of numbers?

....

....

b) There is a special name given to each step in the food chain – what is this name? (Hint: rearrange *Phil Coverlet* to find the two words). Energy is lost going from one organism to the next. Explain why this happens.

....

....

....

SECTION SEVEN — ORGANISMS IN THEIR ENVIRONMENT

Questions on Survival

Q1 *Foxes chase, catch and eat rabbits. Rabbits have features that allow them to run away and escape. The flow chart on the right shows how rabbits have <u>adapted</u> to run fast and escape foxes.*

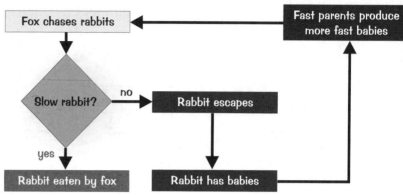

a) Why don't slow rabbits pass on as many of their genes to the next generation?

....

....

....

....

b) Explain why fast rabbits pass on more of their genes to the next generation than slow rabbits.

....

....

....

....

c) Explain why after a few generations, rabbits become more able to escape the fox.

....

....

....

....

d) In a race between a rabbit from a field where there are foxes, and a rabbit from a field without any foxes, which rabbit is more likely to win? Give a reason for your answer.

....

....

....

....

SECTION SEVEN — ORGANISMS IN THEIR ENVIRONMENT

Questions on Survival

Q2a) Design an *ultimate predator* that is good at surviving. Explain how it is adapted to be successful at catching its prey. It can have almost any features you like, but there is one rule – it cannot be invisible!

....

....

....

....

....

....

b) Design an *ultimate prey*. Not an animal that is really easy to catch, but one that is very difficult for a predator to catch and eat, and so is good at surviving. Explain how it is adapted to escape from predators. It can have almost any features you like, but again the same rule – it cannot be invisible!

....

....

....

....

....

....

c) Compare your ultimate predator with your ultimate prey. Do they have any features in common that make them good at surviving? If they do, make a list of these features.

....

....

....

....

....

....

Questions on Survival

Q3 *You have been asked to write the screenplay for a film in which a terrible space alien has crash-landed on Earth. The army is trying to find the alien, but it can change itself to adapt to its surroundings. You need three thrilling scenes, one where the alien is in a forest, one where it is undersea, and one where it is in the desert. For each of these three places, make a list of the features you think the alien would give itself so that it could survive well there.*

Features of the alien for the thrilling forest scenes...

....

....

....

....

....

....

Features of the alien for the rip-roaring undersea scenes...

....

....

....

....

....

....

Features of the alien for the scorching desert scenes...

....

....

....

....

....

....